Around
Burton upon Trent

IN OLD PHOTOGRAPHS

The Rifleman Revellers, a concert party based at the Rifleman Inn, Derby Street, *c*. 1930. They gave charity performances that typified the cameraderie and home-made entertainment often characteristic of old town pubs. The inn has now been converted into a shop.

Around Burton upon Trent

IN OLD PHOTOGRAPHS

Collected by
CEOFFREY SOWERBY *and*
RICHARD FARMAN

Budding BOOKS

This book was first published in 1993 by
Sutton Publishing Limited · Phoenix Mill
Thrupp · Stroud · Gloucestershire · GL5 2BU

This edition first published in 2001 by
Budding Books, an imprint of
Sutton Publishing Limited

Reprinted in 2002, 2004, 2005

British Library Cataloguing in Publication Data
A catalogue record for this book is available from the
British Library

ISBN 1-84015-269-9

Typeset in 9/10 Sabon
Typesetting and origination by
Sutton Publishing Limited.
Printed in Great Britain by
J.H. Haynes & Co. Ltd, Sparkford.

The Dingle, Stapenhill, leading to the Ferry Bridge, was a narrow pathway alongside a stream running down to the river, making it a happy play place for these Victorian children.

Contents

A view across the Trent to Burton, 1860s. The town's rapid development began in the early eighteenth century with the opening of the Trent Navigation and erection of a wharf and warehouses at the Soho. It continued with the coming of the Trent and Mersey Canal in 1770 – though this, in turn, ended the river trade. Burton's greatest expansion, however, followed the opening of the Birmingham to Derby railway in 1839. The Burton, Uttoxeter and Ashbourne Union Bank was established and 1840 saw the introduction of the penny post – all events helping to foster and spread commercial activity.

Introduction

Following the Trent we soon arrive within sight of chimneys, large
buildings, and all the signs of a busy town.
'Why!' you exclaim in astonishment, 'the place is filled with
barrels.'
They are everywhere; piled in pyramids on the ground, stacked on
railway trucks, heaped on drays . . .
And then it dawns on you that you are at Burton.

Glimpses of Greater Britain, ed. Herbert Hayens (Collins, *c.* 1908)

Being invited to contribute to this series of Britain in Old Photographs has
given us the privilege of presenting the biggest single collection of pictures of
Burton upon Trent and district to appear in one volume – over two hundred
and thirty scenes covering the town and the area immediately surrounding it.
We have been able to include many photographs which have not previously
appeared in any local book.

It will be appreciated that with a large number of pictures the amount of
space available for text is, of necessity, limited. Consequently this is not a
history book. Rather, it is a pictorial reflection of aspects of local life in town
and village from the last century right through, in two or three instances, to
the last decade.

The pace of change everywhere continues to accelerate with, for example,
the whole style of local architecture constantly changing as the old gives way
to the new. Whether change is always for the better may be open to argument
but at least we can show in these pages something of what has changed and
recall what has disappeared for ever.

We decided to present this wide-ranging photographic record grouped
under flexible thematic headings so that we look at the town itself and its
industries, as its shops and transport and, briefly, at the impact of the First
World War. We move out to the fringe villages of Staffordshire and then cross
the Trent to take in Stapenhill, Winshill and the closely adjoining areas of
South Derbyshire which, although having much in common with Burton, also
provide great differences and contrasts. Until they were transferred to
Staffordshire for local government purposes in 1894, Stapenhill and Winshill
were Derbyshire villages, the Trent being the ancient geographical and
historical boundary. Above all, however, in making this selection we have tried
to place the emphasis on people (named whenever possible) – their daily lives,

the events and occasions they attended and their individual or group activities and achievements.

Then, of course, there are those who made it all possible in the first place – those who looked through the eye of the camera. The area has been fortunate enough to have a number of very active and capable local photographers to whom we are pleased to pay tribute with this collection. Most prolific were the Simnetts – John, whose photographs date back to the early 1860s and his sons, J.S. and A.J., who, from 1888 until 1950, carried on the business (which still continues under the old name but no longer with family connections). In addition, by reproducing old prints and engravings as photographs the Simnetts have left us views dating back to earlier centuries. This selection includes many and varied examples of their work.

Ernest Abrahams, Richard Keene, F.W. Scarratt of Derby, Siddals of Newhall, Perks of Woodville and others have all made their contributions, while over seventy different publishers sent cameramen to the area at different times for their picture postcards. Local press photographers have subsequently continued recording scenes and events in more recent times, and we are indeed indebted to all who have made it possible to assemble this collection.

For some people this may be a book for memories and nostalgia; for others, perhaps, enlightenment about the local past. We would like to think that some readers may find recollections of families or friends remembered and recorded in these pages. For all, we hope, there will be discovery, interest and enjoyment.

In 1910 a local solicitor, B.C. Newbold, organized the Burton League of Frontiersmen, young volunteers with their own horses who practised military training.

SECTION ONE

Around the Town

Looking over the town from St Paul's church tower, *c.* 1902. St Paul's Street East (foreground) was cleared to create King Edward Place in front of the Town Hall. Properties adjoining the Town Hall were cleared for its extension in the 1930s.

On 23 February 1863 Mr John Richardson, High Bailiff of Burton, laid the first stone for the new Burton bridge. Here the arches can be seen under construction (left) with the old bridge on the right. In the centre is the first Holy Trinity church, which had a tower, and centre left is J. Nunnerley's brewery. He merged with J. Marston in 1888. On the right is the building (still surviving) that became Boddington's brewery and then Spooner's Swan works for fairground equipment.

The widening of Trent Bridge, between 1924 and 1926. Before this improvements had been made at both ends. This scene, looking towards the town, gives some idea of the scale of the operation and shows the trackway erected below the north side.

The construction of St Peter's Bridge, 1984. This was Burton's second road crossing.

The interior of Burton parish church showing decorations for the Harvest Festival, 1875. The most interesting aspect of this scene, however, is that it records the old three-decker pulpit and the box pews, long since removed.

Ivy House, Abbey Street. This was demolished in 1954 to make way for Technical College workshops. Former residence of Charrington's head brewer, in 1930 it became the vicarage for Christ Church. The original Christ Church vicarage was not used after the Zeppelin raid of 31 January 1916, when six people died in the parish room.

Lichfield Street, 1904. The cyclist is approaching the town centre but everything appearing here has gone. Butcher Eaton's meat hangs over the pavement, while beyond were a tobacconist, the New Inn, a hairdresser, shoeing smith, fishmonger and grocer. Opposite, in contrast, were large houses belonging to the professional classes (there is one survivor, No. 50), but then came a sequence of six properties, perhaps unique even for Burton, comprising four pubs, an off-licence and Charrington's brewery, which stood on the present B & Q site alongside the Leopard Inn.

Before the opening of the Ferry Bridge in 1889 a penny ferry boat took passengers across the Trent at Stapenhill. Carte-de-visite photographs were used for views as well as portraits before the advent of picture postcards.

The viaduct during flooding, December 1910. This and the Ferry Bridge were among Lord Burton's gifts to the town. Crossing the Trent could be like a walk on the pier, as illustrated here.

Station Street from High Street immediately before total demolition and rebuilding, 1901. Mrs Christian, the newsagent, is still in business but A.J. Roberts, pork butcher (later of Roberts and Birch) has gone – note his ventilated shutters – and so has Mr Walker, also a butcher. The yard of Charles Salt, shoeing smith, came next, while Ordish and Hall were having a big sale before moving to fine new premises. Two old cottages had lasted without being turned into shops.

Another view of old Station Street properties looking back towards High Street, *c.* 1901. W.J. Read, corn, cake and meal merchant, resumed trading at the rear of rebuilt premises (No. 14) until the 1930s and moved later to Bank Square and the Market Hall, where he specialized in all kinds of bird food. The posters make a fascinating social study today, even if a ladder might have been helpful then for reading some of them!

A Simnett photograph of an etching recording Burton's windmill, which stood in the area behind the present Station Hotel. When erected in 1818 it was at the end of Derby Lane, subsequently Derby Street. Early millers were John Stonier and Thomas Buxton. When demolished in 1891 it was owned by George Read & Son, who were also working the Granville (steam) mill, Swadlincote.

The Star, an old Burton inn (originally the Star of Bethlehem), 1888. This inn has survived after rebuilding and renaming. The sketch shows the shop of Dawson and Howarth (1863) and what was the post office building from 1877 to 1905 and is now the Constitutional Club.

Dame Paulet's Almshouses (1593) in Bank Square fell victim to redevelopment. The door arch is now on the wall of Littlewood's Store, with its erroneous re-cut inscription. The first two letters of Anno Domini having worn off, a local mason, not knowing Latin, engraved it symmetrically as NO DOMI NI.

Station Street as redeveloped, photographed from the top of Boots the Chemist, *c.* 1910. Both closed and open trams are operating and a few early cars appear among the horse traffic.

The Devonshire Arms, 1860s. At this date the pub still had its garden and fields around it although Station Street was rapidly being developed with newly laid out streets branching off it.

Burton's first infirmary opened in October 1869 in Duke Street, financed by public subscription. A larger building replaced it in 1899. Further extensions were added and opened in 1942.

Looking across Trent Bridge before widening. The old public baths, left, closed on 9 March 1980. Built in 1873 they were donated by the Ratcliff family. Little of the once distinctive skyline beyond now remains.

Bridge Street decorated for Queen Victoria's Diamond Jubilee, 1897. Heath's shop then stood on Wetmore Road corner; next to the Queen's Hotel was the Saracen's Head, Maxted (tailor and habit maker) and several professional chambers, including three surgeons. The house on the extreme right belonged to T.N. Whitehead, town clerk, and was demolished in the 1920s for bridge widening. His remarkable gravestone in Burton cemetery traces his ancestry back to the early kings of England.

This is the first George Street Methodist chapel of 1852, which was already too small by 1860 when the present chapel replaced it. The open space seen here became the site in 1867 for St George's Hall, which in turn became the Opera House, the Ritz Cinema, the Gaumont and now the Odeon.

A rare scene showing the interior of a Burton public house. This is the Wheatsheaf Inn on the High Street/Station Street corner, now converted to shops. It was favoured by touring theatrical companies and also staged its own entertainment – for example, 'Expensive engagement of superior artistes' for Bank Holiday Monday 1907, along with 'The local child marvel, Annie Bramley' (in centre), shown here in 1921 with her stepmother Alice and her son Ted. She was the daughter of landlord Harry (Sam) Bramley.

Work in High Street for the opening of the tramways, 3 August 1903. On the left is Hallams, chemists, established in 1768. Next is Ordish and Hall's new building, replacing premises in Station Street that were demolished along with Philadelphia Corner, the old building seen beyond it. The Wheatsheaf Inn is seen across the junction with Station Street.

Flooding in the High Street, 22 October 1875. There were two severe floods in this year that inundated main streets in the town, the second providing this view. It shows the old post office where John Whitehurst was postmaster, which opened from 7.30 a.m. to 10 p.m. with letters dispatched to all parts at 11 p.m.

Horninglow Street, 23 May 1932. A Stevenson's bus splashes past No. 56, where Mrs Webb recorded: 'The occupants of these three houses (55, 56, 57) and the Public on the corner lived upstairs on this date. 10½ inches of water inside. Oh, what a mess!' The 'Public' was the Union Tavern on the corner of Brook Street. This was an area always liable to flood, and a stone let into a wall nearby recorded the much higher level reached in 1875.

Workers' cottages at the rear of Guild Street, just before demolition, 1976. This is one of many rows of cottages, little noticed and seldom recorded, situated behind most of Burton's town centre streets. New Street had Courts 3, 4, 5, 7, 9 and 10 well into this century; Station Street had Albert Place with thirty-two small houses that only disappeared in the 1930s; Congreve Buildings (down a passage between Nos 177 and 178) lasted until the 1960s. Backing on to Bass's cooperage, these cottages were numbered 66a to 70a and stood behind 66–70 Guild Street.

Burton Boys' Grammar School moved to Bond Street from Friar's Walk in 1877. The headmaster's house was damaged in the 1916 air raid and subsequently adapted for school use. When the new grammar school opened at Winshill in 1957 the technical college used the vacated premises, but all have now gone.

The Railway Mission Hall by Moor Street crossing was opened by Lady Burton in 1904. Earlier meetings were held on Burton station. Smith's bookstall produced this view of the simple interior. Later the Elim Church used this hall before acquiring the redundant Christ Church building.

Mrs. Steel and all Workers greet you this Xmas Day, and wish you well.

INFANT WELFARE CENTRE,
BURTON-ON-TRENT.

In 1911 there were twenty-eight local midwives and most babies were born at home, often without the mother ever seeing a doctor. The appointment that year of a lady health visitor and the opening of an infant welfare centre at 55 Union Street were thus great advances in health care and provision.

Wards in the second infirmary building, decorated for Christmas 1908. This was built in 1899 in the area between Duke Street and New Street.

A new isolation hospital was built at Outwoods in the 1890s to replace the old one in Horninglow Street. The Outwoods site in turn became part of the new district hospital complex.

New Street Baptist chapel under repair in the mid-1930s provides an example of the elaborate wooden scaffolding of the period. F.H. Appleby & Son of Queen Street were well-known local builders, C.H. Appleby, the son, now being in charge. Fire destroyed the chapel in 1966, and demolition followed. The site is now a shop and car park.

The Picturedrome, now used for bingo, began as a rolling skating rink but by 1914 had become a picture house. It was completely rebuilt in eight months in 1931 as a new super-cinema seating nearly two thousand people.

SECTION TWO

People and Events

Sunday 20 June 1897 saw thanksgiving services held for Queen Victoria's Diamond Jubilee. On Monday there was a rather unsuccessful ox-roast – but 'more beef was generously provided so the poor did not lose their feast'. This scene is of Tuesday's open air service outside the parish church. Twenty thousand people later attended a free fête and at 10 p.m. bonfires were lit. Wednesday was Children's Day, over ten thousand assembling for 'a substantial meal' followed by sports! Elderly people had tea and entertainment on the Friday.

King Edward VII's visit to Burton, 22 February 1902. He was staying at Rangemore Hall with Lord Burton. His Majesty visited the Bass brewery and these arches in Forest Road heralded his approach to the town, though not much could be done about the roadway. In Shobnall school yard two thousand children sang the National Anthem as the King drove past.

A group from St John's church, Horninglow, scything the churchyard early this century.

Typical of the grand processions organized for big public occasions is this one for King George V's coronation, 1911. It is taken from near the Wesleyan chapel in Station Street, with a decorated tram (on the right) acting as a grandstand in Guild Street, the old police station just beyond it. It is Thursday 22 June and the civic procession left the Town Hall at 11.30 a.m. for a thanksgiving service in the market-place. This scene focuses on the Church Lads' Brigade and the Boy Scouts with fire brigades following.

MARQUIS OF ANGLESEY

Most photographs of the 5th Marquis of Anglesey emphasize his eccentricities. The family had long associations with Burton and were ground landlords of large parts of the town. The Marquis's activities aroused great interest locally: his extravagant way of life, his collection of jewellery, his performances at home and abroad, dancing in exotic costumes, and his theatre company with which he toured playing leading roles. He succeeded to the title in 1896, dying in Paris in 1905.

In contrast, the 6th Marquis of Anglesey was active in Burton affairs, serving as mayor in 1911/12. This elaborate silver casket was presented to him, with the freedom of the Borough, on the occasion of his marriage to Lady Marjorie Manners, 3 August 1912.

Burton Leander Rowing Club were particularly successful during the Edwardian era, and were coached by J.J. Auber. The Senior Coxed Four display their trophies for 1909.

A clerical occasion at St Paul's church when former vicars and curates joined the incumbent, the Revd J.J. Stockley, on St Paul's Day, 1905. This church was built by M.T. Bass, Lord Burton's father, in 1874.

Salem Baptist church group, *c.* 1910. Standing, left to right: Mrs Blackwell, Messrs James, Lewis, Inger, Wall, Martin, Mrs Inger, Mr Fidkin, Revd David Donald, Mr Blackwell, Mr H. Lewis, Mrs R. Inger. Seated: Mr Lowood, Mrs Martin, Mr Smith, Mrs Smith, Mr Cotton, Mrs Moore. Their church in Station Street was built in 1803 and rebuilt in 1861 and 1957.

In 1903 Miss Annie Boulton and Miss Ethel Tresise trained these seventy youngsters for highly successful concerts at George Street chapel and Stapenhill Institute, where this photograph was taken. A programme of the words has also been discovered to complete the record. One up-to-the-minute item is of some social interest. Entitled 'The Motor Car', verse one painted an idyllic country scene, verse two told of sudden noise and smell, and in verse three 'the ugly monster' exploded.

Bass offices decorated for the coronation of King Edward VII, 1902. The archway was over the brewery entrance and at night the High Street frontage was illuminated by naked gas lights.

The Corporation Gas Department illuminated the Town Hall for the coronation of King George V, 1911. The profiles on the side wall were also made up of gas pipes and lit up at night. The Town Hall extension was subsequently added on this side.

ꓑew . .
Theatre and
Opera ꓧouse,
BURTON.

Proprietors—
Mr. WILLIAM BENNETT.
Mr. H. G. DUDLEY BENNETT.

Acting Manager—
Mr. COOKE FRANKISH.

Opening Night, 17th November, 1902.

Prospective Engagements.

View of Proscenium.

Christmas—
" Kitty Grey."
Jan. 5th—
" Country Girl."
Jan. 12th—
Pantomime.
Jan. 19th—
" Sporting Life."
Jan. 26th—
" La Poupee."
Feb. 2nd—
Pantomime.
Feb 9th—
Pantomime.
Feb. 16th—
" Floradora."

Unique views of the interior of Burton Opera House, which opened with a performance of *Faust* by the Moody Manners Company. They presented a repertoire of six operas during the first week.

Burton Opera House staff outside the main entrance in George Street. The play *My Son John* on the poster dates this to the week of 22 October 1928. Fourth from right, front row, is Mr J.W. Wright – who worked at the theatre from 1902, when it opened, until closure in 1934.

During Burton Aviation Week in 1910 the Opera House staged the musical comedy *A Chinese Honeymoon*. The aviators and theatre company combined for this photograph outside the Liberal Club in George Street. Seated centre with her male colleagues is the pioneer lady flyer, Mademoiselle Hélène Dutrieu.

The Grange Lawn Tennis Club, off St Paul's Square, dated from 1885 and was the largest and socially the leading local club in 1904, when this group of members was photographed.

Lifeboat parades formed up in St Paul's Street. This fancy dress party poses with the local National Union of Railwaymen's banner depicting the Burton coat of arms, M.T. Bass Esq., and a Midland Railway engine loading Burton Ale.

The annual lifeboat procession, 26 June 1909. During this event an obsolete boat was drawn through the town by brewery horses while money was collected. Against a backdrop of breweries the boat was then launched from The Hay into the Trent.

Burton YMCA premises at 163 High Street, now demolished. This is the formal opening ceremony, which was performed by the Marquess of Northampton. In the centre is the mayor, J.R. Morris; on his right the towering figure of the Revd W.F. Drury, Vicar of Holy Trinity. Bailey's Refreshment Rooms adjoin with their ornate external window lighting, while the hall and gymnasium entrance benefit from the splendid gas lamp.

Major R.F. Ratcliff (subsequently Colonel Ratcliff) was Member of Parliament for the town from 1900 until 1918. He was Commanding Officer of the Burton Volunteer Companies of the 6th Battalion (Prince of Wales) North Staffordshire Regiment. A director of Bass, Ratcliff and Gretton, he played a prominent role in the local community.

In 1906 Burton's sitting Member of Parliament, Major Ratcliff, was opposed for the Liberals by Captain F.P. Fletcher-Vane. Neither local nor a brewer, he added to his problems, according to one of the down-to-earth press reports of the day, when he 'made a simple but quite unnecessary confession . . . by saying that he was not a speaker. The fact is palpable to the most unobservant mind after listening for a few minutes to his laboured utterances.'

The Clement family, 1915. They were all talented musicians: Walter was an Opera House pianist and his brother George, with two daughters and son, seen here, provided improvised music for silent films at the Electric Theatre.

Guild Street School was also used for evening classes. A group poses in the rear yard, which later housed scenery workshops for the Municipal School of Speech and Drama. Started in 1946, this was the first school of its kind to be run by a small local authority. This much earlier group appear to be budding plumbers.

The Drama School's Little Theatre enjoyed many years of success under George Draper, George Makin and its final principal, Ronald Whetton. It was also used by dramatic societies and other groups, and this scene is from Geoffrey Sharp's Coronation Revue *Midsummer Madness*, 1953. Left to right: Maurice Smalley, Jean Barton, Geoffrey Sowerby, Doris Campbell, John Kelly, Valerie Sharp, Jack Ricketts, Joan Pumford.

The Church Lads' Brigade was active locally before the Scout movement. It catered for the 13 to 19 age group, and combined military and physical drill with Bible classes. The scene shows clearing up after the annual camp, 1904.

An early local scout group, c. 1912. They certainly sport the long shorts then in favour. It is believed to be Mr S.J. Fisher, schoolmaster, in charge.

Fashionably dressed, these ladies were delegates at the Twenty-fifth Anniversary Congress of the Women's Co-operative Guild at Burton Town Hall, June 1908. The Guild had 500 branches and 25,500 members.

These students from the Pupil Teachers' Centre in Wellington Street are attired for a May festival in 1908. The centre operated from 1907 until 1914, when this training system fell out of Government favour.

The Burton and District Football Association was formed in 1871 at the Rising Sun, Horninglow Street, and is claimed as the country's oldest Association. Here is a typical team photograph recalling a side that enjoyed its heyday in the early 1920s. All Saints played on the Crescent Ground, their Secretary being T.A. Richins. They were local Division One Champions in 1921–2 and again in 1922–3, when they also swept the Cup competitions. Back row, left to right: Langley, Harriss, Clarke, Maskrey, Nicklin, Goldby. Front row: Muggleston, Reddington, Parker, Clarke, Riley.

Lord Burton was born at the Bass town house, 136 High Street, on 12 November 1837, and died at his London residence, Chesterfield House, on 1 February 1909.

Drapes fall from the Lord Burton statue in King Edward Place at the unveiling by the Earl of Dartmouth, Lord-Lieutenant of Staffordshire, 13 May 1911. Thousands gathered to honour the town's principal benefactor.

On 23 July 1929 HRH the Prince of Wales (later King Edward VIII) arrived by aeroplane at Bass's meadow to visit the town. After a Town Hall luncheon he toured the Bass brewery and appears here with Mr P.W. Ratcliff, one of the directors. He visited the war memorial, 'inspected' three thousand school children, went to the Branston Artificial Silk Company, the Infirmary and the India Rubber, Gutta Percha and Telegraph Works Co. Ltd, before departing after tea at the Drill Hall.

THOMAS JENKINS ESQ
(HON: SECY: & TRES:)
PRIMROSE LEAGUE DEMONSTRATION

SIR ROBERT GRESLEY BART
(CHAIRMAN)
AT DRAKELOWE

A Primrose League demonstration at Drakelow Hall, ancestral home of the Gresleys, 27 July 1907. The League was dedicated to the maintenance of religion, the estates of the realm and the imperial ascendancy of Great Britain – principles advocated by Disraeli, whose favourite flower was the primrose. At this time the League enjoyed wide local support. T. Jenkins, a Burton architect and later mayor, is talking to Sir Robert Gresley on the terrace. The hall was demolished in 1934 and in 1954 Drakelow power station was built on the site.

'Still life' was often employed for local souvenir postcards. Here the *Burton Observer* shows scenes from Burton Operatic Society's 1933 production of *Dorothy* at the Opera House. Florence Chandler played the lead; the conductor was H.J. Cumper, prominent singer and musician; and photographer J.S. Simnett was stage manager.

St Modwen's parish churchyard has become the Memorial Gardens, the old gravestones now assembled together in avenues. Among them is that of 'Dumb Tom', with its poignant inscription telling how it came to be raised in memory of Tom Stokes, a local character who was both deaf and dumb.

One of Burton's early photographers was George Renwick, winner of many medals and certificates. The identity of the little girl in this charming Victorian portrait is, unfortunately, not known.

Some of these early keep-fit enthusiasts have vests inscribed YLPCC, believed to be the Youth League Physical Culture Club, but records of its activities are elusive.

A 1920s portrait from photographer J.S. Simnett's own studio. Albert Simnett, his brother, cycled round collecting instalment money for photographs supplied. His son told of his hasty retreat when a maidservant wanted a nude photograph of herself on the drawing-room sofa in the family's absence.

Fourteen members of Burton Grammar School Old Boys Rugby XV, December 1931. They were playing the school XV on the Memorial Ground at Peel Croft, where the now demolished Park Street maltings form the background. Back row, left to right: Dai Davies, Vernon Moore, Ben Ward, John Hipwell, 'Tuf' Williams, Arthur Kirby, Stan Ife. Front row: Bert Sorton; ? McLennon, Ron Kenning, Rupert Sims, Charlie Smith, Jack Burdett, Stan Snead.

SECTION THREE

Breweries and Industry

When the Ancient Order of Foresters held their High Court at Burton in 1911, social events included tours of Bass's brewery. Visitors pose with a typical background of barrels, the internal rail transport and sacks of hops; these are from mid-Kent.

222054.J.V.   BASS & C?'S BREWERY, BURTON-ON-TRENT.

A Bass brewery scene, once typical of views from town centre streets but all now swept away. We see one of the Guild Street level crossings, grain warehouses and overhead walkway, vans and open trucks, one of Bass's own engines, a floater loaded with barrels, the water tower, even the worker with his wicker lunch basket – all just memories – captured in this one splendid photograph. The view looks down Middle Yard towards High Street, with the old Store Room on the left, later used as a malt store, and No. 2 barley drying kiln on the right. The crossing gates remained hand operated.

Every year Burton breweries recruited additional workers for the malting season. They were mainly agricultural labourers from East Anglia who worked from September until Easter while farm work was slack. They were traditionally known as 'norkies' and often found lodgings with local brewery workers, one of whom is posing here in the centre. These two 'norkies', with malt shovel and rake, are working for Bass's – who engaged some two hundred and fifty extra workers at the turn of the century.

'Trussing out' was a traditional ritual at breweries when a coopering apprentice finished his time. After having ale and wood shavings tipped over him, he would be rolled around in a barrel that he had completed himself.

'The Merry Party' appear on this early Edwardian scene that shows a corner of a small cooperage. The men are wearing the traditional barm cloth aprons and surrounded by tools relating to their trade.

This is Allsopp's Racking Room, pre-1914. The barrels were collected in 'racking squares' to be filled, men sounding them with wooden mallets to check that this had been done. Filled casks received a handful of best hops to add the final flavour. Bungs were closed with hammers, and the 'marker' stamped each cask with date, brew number and ale quality. It was possible for eight men to fill, bung and roll away 400 casks per hour.

Many early brewery locomotives were built in Burton by Thornewill and Warham. This example, Bass No. 4, supplied in 1872, is seen in the Middle Brewery in 1887. This photograph was used for an engraving in Alfred Barnard's *Noted Breweries of Great Britain and Ireland* (1889).

Bass ale for the forces during the First World War. Women packers are putting quart bottles into wooden crates, each holding six dozen and marked 'for Rouen'.

A view of Bass's hop weighing room, everything meticulously clean and orderly, showing scales, hand trolleys and 'jiggers' for wheeling pockets of hops around easily.

Shobnall maltings showing the extent of the Bass malthouses (1873–6) and the complex of rail connections providing for exchange traffic between internal and main lines.

Marston, Thompson and Evershed brewery from the air showing their rail connection coming in over the Trent and Mersey Canal. Their sports ground adjoins on the right. The lines in the foreground served Ind Coope maltings, now demolished. In the distance can be seen a Bass pumping station and the extensive 'Klondyke' sidings, which catered for Bass's Shobnall maltings, their bottling and ale stores and cask washing premises.

The Bass fire brigade, pre-1921. Here are two Merryweather steamers, a manual pump and a personnel carrier. Eight horses were kept on stand-by and the volunteer firemen worked in the nearby premises belonging to the Engineer's Department. This unique building curved alongside a railway line. In 1921 the first motor engines were acquired.

Peach's maltings in Wood Street were seriously damaged in one of Burton's biggest fires, July 1908. Smouldering grain required the presence of a fire crew for several weeks.

Henry Wardle, head of Salt's brewery, served as MP for South Derbyshire. He had the distinction of twice being called upon to read the Riot Act – in Swadlincote in 1864 and in Burton in 1878 – following disturbances after the first municipal elections.

Worthington's 1896 Hudswell Clarke 0–4–0 shunter No. 3. It became Bass No. 12 in 1954 and was disposed of in 1958. The extra large buffers ensured contact when wagons were being shunted round tight curves.

William Henry Worthington (1826–94), head of the brewing firm, was chairman of the Town Commissioners in 1878 when the town was made a municipal borough and became first mayor of Burton upon Trent, serving from 1878 to 1879.

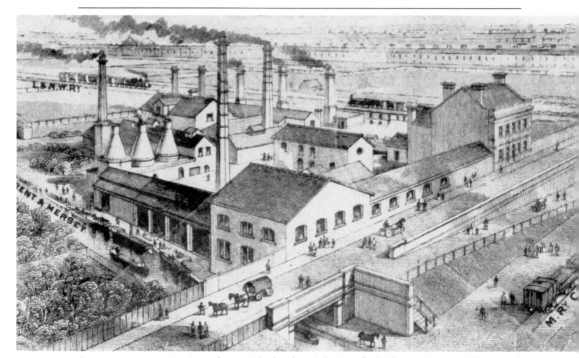

A unique panoramic view of a vanished industrial site, of which no photographic record has come to light. Now built over, the only traces remaining are the bridge under which the London and North Western Railway gained access to Burton, and what was, in effect, a new viaduct (*c.* 1874) taking Shobnall Road over the railway and the Trent and Mersey Canal with Staton's Cement Works in between. Note the plaster and cement kilns and canal loading dock. The Midland Railway (on the right) ran a line along the bed of the former Bond End canal.

Gas was first used locally in 1832 from a works on the Station Street/Union Street corner before being re-established at Wetmore and coming under town control after 1854. Some small village undertakings were later taken over. Handcarts like this were once a familiar sight, with over 2,000 street lamps to be maintained.

Products of a small iron-founding company, which also specialized in manufacturing abrasives. Pollett's Waterloo Street works was cleared to make way for the Town Hall car park. Originally Buxton and Thornley, engineers, produced the 'Burton' steam pump on this site.

The Swan works of C.J. Spooner off Trent Bridge. He was noted for fairground apparatus and caravans and the skilful wood-carving and painting associated with them. Combining with G. Orton he set up the Orton and Spooner works in Victoria Crescent, which closed in 1981. The building seen here had been Boddington's and then Everard's brewery. An arch of Burton's medieval bridge remains as part of a cellar.

The Hull fair, 1904. This splendid structure for wax-works and bioscope is a classic example of Spooner carving and gilding.

Two fairground horses carved by Spooner before their dispatch by rail. Note the Staffordshire Knot symbol on the North Staffs Railway wagon in one of Burton's many goods yards.

Councillor Charles Tresise was mayor of Burton from 1907 to 1909. His family firm of printers, publishers, stationers and newspaper proprietors was established in 1859. Tresise's printing business continues to thrive today.

An early view of the Pirelli tyre factory, Derby Road, established in 1929 when new local industry was being encouraged by offers of land, sewerage, gas and electricity at specially favourable rates.

The Branston Pickle factory, with its internal railway system, during Messrs Crosse and Blackwell's occupancy. Someone has obligingly indicated the vinegar brewery and the pickle shop, which have been described as 'aromatic', but when artificial silk manufacture took over in 1927 a more massive chimney, 360 ft high, was erected to disperse fumes. It was spectacularly demolished in 1937.

Ind Coope introduced their beers into Belgium with a stand at the Commercial Fair in Brussels in 1920. The Belgian agent here receives congratulations from His Majesty, the King of the Belgians.

A unique example of the cask labels that were pasted on the heads of Burton Brewery Company barrels. Always washed off when casks were cleaned, this survivor is a sample label from a printer's proof book acknowledging an order to supply 10,000 labels, dark blue in colour, and is dated 15 October 1857. The Burton Brewery Company (1842) was eventually acquired by Worthington's in 1914.

SECTION FOUR

Shopping and Advertising

Oakden's Grocery, 1906. A noted Burton shop, it opened in 1770 and traded until the 1950s. W.S. Oakden was living over the shop at this date and his private entrance can be seen on the right. A handsome medal was awarded to him that year at the Grocery, Provision, Oil and Italian Warehouse and Allied Trades Exhibition and Market.

Opposite St Peter's church, Stapenhill Road, August 1914. Hoardings were a feature round the town, often positioned with little regard for any environmental effect: this one was on a residential road and left little room for pedestrians between it and the tram lines. A public meeting on 2 September in response to Lord Kitchener's Appeal is advertised, there is 'Latest War News' in the *Evening Telegraph*, while *England Expects* is showing at the Electric Theatre. For relaxation David Devant's magic is at the Hippodrome (Opera House) and The Parisians are at the Anglesey Palace in Friars' Walk.

Darley's bookshop, 1928. It had opened in 1827 and closed in June 1963. The shop was demolished together with the printing works, which moved to new premises. Burton's first library was here, and the firm also published postcards and pioneered the printing of beer bottle labels. Below is one of their advertising envelopes.

Like most towns Burton once abounded with small shopkeepers 'open all hours' and selling a wide range of items. Reuben Guilford, by trade a fitter, ran his little shop at 55 Calais Road in the 1920s. No stylish window dressing here – a few vegetables outside (including Batchelor's peas); within, everything from Hudson's soap to Colman's starch and Radiance toffee to Woodbine cigarettes.

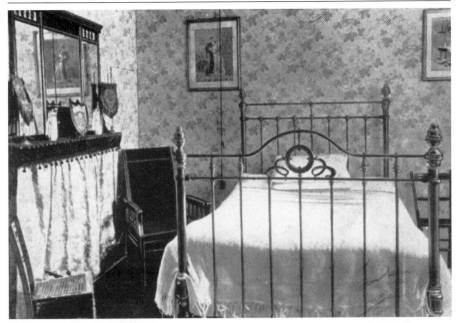

A single room at the Queen's Hotel, 1912. This room cost 3s, while a double room cost 4s 6d and private sitting rooms cost half a crown (2s 6d). A leading commercial hotel, originally the Three Queens, it dated back to 1531 and was a posting house in coaching days.

In mid-Edwardian days tram-cars and bicycles provided the commonest wheeled transport. In the town centre George Povey's dining rooms on the market-place corner specifically advertised 'Accommodation For Cyclists'.

Several photographs of Freer's, newsagents in Derby Street, show elaborate advertising. This particular week it was for Cassell's Publications, including their 'Popular Sheet Music' (over the entrance) at 2*d* each, while even space under the doorstep is used. A publisher's representative would assist with these special displays. Mr J.J. Freer is in the doorway, and his daughter and granddaughter still serve in this shop today.

This is the same shop without a special display, Wednesday 4 October 1905. The date is indicated by the newspaper posters. One sensational news story of the day concerned developments over the murder of Miss Money on 24 September in Mertsham tunnel on the Brighton line. Picture postcards figure prominently in the window.

Morning paper delivery boys pose in front of Burton station platform bookstall at 7.20 a.m., each provided with W.H. Smith cap, cape and bike.

The Co-op favoured quiet dignity at their outfitting department, 255–6 Waterloo Street. The Society had branches and departments all around the town and the surrounding district, and eventually had thirty branch shops.

A typical Co-op branch shop (number seven of thirty) in South Broadway Street. It was moved to Branston Road before the First World War.

Licensing legislation was, predictably, of much local concern – as reflected in topical advertising, 1908. A Liberal bill aimed at reducing the total number of licensed premises around the country. It was defeated in the House of Lords and in Burton even most Liberals opposed it. Smith's the dyers remained in business until the 1930s.

Looking into the boot-making and repairing workshop of Joseph Locker at 58–9 New Street, *c.* 1907. His advertising stressed his 'cleverest of clever workmen' and warned against the 'humbug of "Multiple" or "Company" shops', his repairs being more promptly and skilfully performed. H. Locker, his son, ran a similar business in Waterloo Street.

As well as styling himself a 'Practical Hatter,' Starkey Berry of 5 High Street offered a fine selection of shirts with detachable collars, and many pairs of British Argosy braces!

Many local concert parties and schools of dance performed between the wars. Here, youngsters from the school run by Amy and Reuben Edgeley are advertising their sponsor, in the early 1920s. Their two-hour Saturday morning classes cost 1s.

Midland Railway horse-drawn express parcels delivery vans provided mobile advertising – one of these, surprisingly, commending Hastings and St Leonard's. There was, in fact, a through Midland service at this time, (c. 1904) in conjunction with the southern railway companies.

The Little Dustpan was a popular general and furnishing store, established in 1879. The unusual building seen here dated from 1907 but was the victim of this serious fire in 1913. One of Burton's leading photographers was Ernest Abrahams, son of the proprietor.

G. Henson & Co. Ltd of Parker Street (established 1867) were aerated water manufacturers and bottlers of ales, stouts and cider, being early users of the then new Crown Cork system for sealing bottles. They introduced a popular Victorian non-alcoholic beverage, 'Phospherine'.

Sanders Brothers premises, St Peter's Street, 1900. They are still recognizable today but at this time Sanders were producing all kinds of horse-drawn vehicles to order for domestic and agricultural use. They also had a workshop at Rolleston.

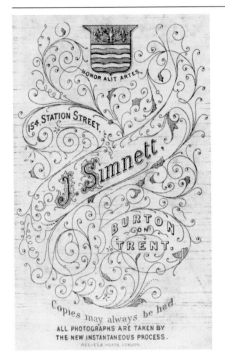

A carte-de-visite by J. Simnett, founder of the photographic firm, at 154 Station Street. He moved to 76 Guild Street in the 1880s, while J.S. Simnett moved to 4 Guild Street in 1900. The design incorporates the borough coat of arms.

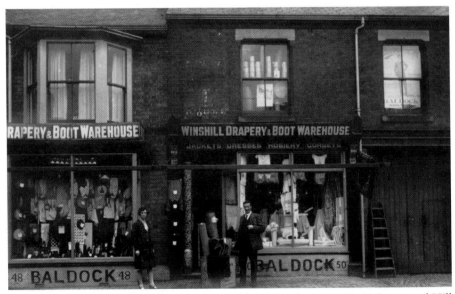

Until around 1930 Winshill had a drapery and boot warehouse at 48–50 Bearwood Hill Road, where Albert Baldock stocked a wide range of goods. Now private houses, original fittings for gas lighting over the windows can still be seen.

SECTION FIVE

Travel and Transport

A smart team of removal men with their horse-drawn van. W.G. Ashforth (formerly Ashforth and Tresise) operated from 136 Derby Street and advertised his competent packers. Note the foreman's little black bag.

A horse bus service, 1899. This is the Horninglow to Market Place (via Victoria Crescent) omnibus, a twenty-minute journey. The driver is John Edward Kent, who, after 1903, worked for the Tramways Department. The stalls are Ronde's Ice Cream and 'Chippy' Heap. The Heaps sold fish and chips here for fifty-three years, until 1940.

The lock on the Trent and Mersey Canal at Dallow Bridge, where the London and North Western Railway had a goods wharf. Canal traffic early this century justified a full-time lock keeper (William Hill) whose house stands between canal and railway.

Burton once had three motor manufacturers: Ryknield, who also made lorries and buses, Salmon and Baguley. The latter took over Salmon cars but became better known for light locomotives. The Salmon works was near Peel Croft, Burton Rugby Club's ground.

An early motoring enthusiast, Mr Ernest Langford of Stapenhill, built this tiller-steered, three-wheeler car – with the registration number FA 14 – early in the century. Employed at the Thornewill and Warham engineering works, he was also a keen racing cyclist.

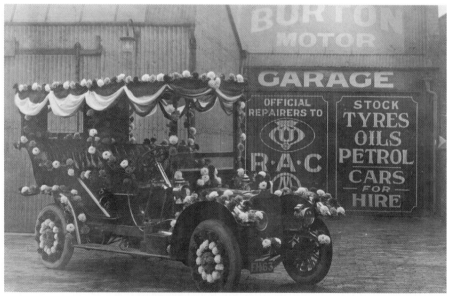

G.F. Reading established his garage in 1902 behind the White Hart Hotel. His brother owned FA 1, a Wolseley, the first vehicle registered by the Burton authority. The car shown is decorated for a local gala.

Looking from Union Street into Guild Street, *c.* 1904. An outing is loading outside the Wesleyan Chapel (demolished in the 1950s), with summer finery on display. Opposite, on Guild Street Corner, is the old police station, then photographer Simnett's shop and the Opera House stage entrance.

First registered in April 1906, FA 113 was listed by the clerk as a Daimler 'charabang'! A 1½-ton public conveyance it loads (overloads?) outside the Navigation Inn, Horninglow Road, with the LNWR embankment in the background. The owner was Percy Bentley, who also had a jewellers shop at 161 Waterloo Street.

Bearwood Hill, showing the sharp curve where the runaway below left the lines – straightened when Trent Bridge was widened. The chimney belonged to Elijah Wigley's saw mill. Newton Road post office, complete with clock, remained until the 1980s.

Tram accident, 8 October 1919. Burton to Ashby tram No. 19 ran back down Bearwood Hill and overturned at the bottom. The conductress, Lillian Parker, and a passenger died, and sixteen people were injured.

An Ashby Light Railways tram leaves High Bank Road, using track laid by Burton Corporation but not used by their cars. Ashby Road, left, still has open fields alongside it and a view over the town. The Waterloo Inn stands alone behind brick walls.

A rare view of track construction between High Bank Road and Bretby Lane. The building (right) was the former toll house. It was moved here from Bearwood Hill when Ashby Road was excavated in 1835–7.

'Success To The Town' is the theme displayed on the Corporation tramcar decorated for the coronation of King George V, 1911. The scene is Horninglow Street depot, where hourly pay at the time for conductors and cleaners was just over £1 for a 54-hour week.

Still standing in Jerram's Lane at the approach to Ferry Bridge is this junction box, sited where trams never ran but recalling the Corporation Tramways system.

The last four trams added to the Burton fleet were Nos 21 to 24 in 1919. With their covered tops removed they were sold to York in 1930. This car, No. 22, became the only Corporation tram to have a serious accident, a broken axle causing it to overturn in Station Street outside the Staffordshire Knot.

Breweries and contractors used steam wagons. Sentinel R8428 belonged to Clark's of Tutbury, and here Dick Allsopp and ? Shaw are in charge.

An impressive line-up of horse power, with a team from the Great Northern Railway handling a heavy boiler outside their goods depot off Hawkins Lane, *c.* 1900.

Horninglow station (built 1883) on Derby Road survived after the line to Tutbury was lifted. A typical example of North Staffordshire railway architecture, it finished its days as a café.

Tutbury's quite impressive station, *c.* 1913, complete with bookstall and the inevitable milk churns.

The 'Tutbury Jenny' made its last run from Burton on 11 June 1960 at 8.12 p.m., with Driver H. Wildgust and Fireman Eric Gorton. John Jennings MP saw the train off. It returned with about five hundred passengers, including co-author Richard Farman, whose bugle-blowing is still recalled and who took his chalk with him to keep in practice for writing!

A Burton station staff photograph in Midland Railway days. As well as the station master, headgear denotes a duty policeman, guard, ticket inspector and two youngsters from the refreshment rooms. Amid drastic changes the station staircase remains little altered today.

On shed at Burton roundhouse in LMS days is 0–6–0 tank engine No. 1607, ex-Midland Railway. Usually about a dozen of this class were allocated to Burton, primarily handling interchange traffic between the main line and brewery private railways.

Horninglow Street, shortly after the Burton and Ashby Light Railways trams ceased to run in 1927. With the rails no longer in use motor buses were able to line up here prior to the opening of the Wetmore Bus Park by the Corporation. At the front is Blue Bus NU 6959, a twenty-eight-seater Halley on the Burton to Derby via Repton route; a small Victoria bus and a Trent bus also running to Derby are behind it. There is a Corporation tram in Bridge Street, the last one running from Winshill on New Year's Eve, 1929.

Burton Aviation Meeting, one of the earliest events of its kind in Britain, was held on
Bass's Meadows from 26 September to 1 October 1910 with a team of French aviators.
Here we see Paul de Lesseps in his Blériot. Navigational errors, obliging him to make
landings at Nottingham and Lichfield, made good publicity and brought many people
to Burton by special trains to watch the flying.

There were great developments in the size and design of aircraft in the three years following the 1910 meeting, but flying was no longer quite such a novelty and the Avro event in August 1913 attracted less attention. This time the airmen were all British: Sydney Pickles (Blériot), Snowdon Hedley (Farman biplane), E. Ronald Whitehouse (Handley Page – conveyed each way by rail) and Mr Raynham's Avro biplane seen here. The occasion caused complaints about disturbance from an unofficial flight, which was made 'during divine service' on the Sunday!

Until 1931 Baguley locomotives – steam, diesel and petrol – were built at the former Ryknield motor works at Shobnall. Construction was then transferred to Uxbridge Street where this engine posed for its official photograph before going to Messrs Wakefield, the oil company.

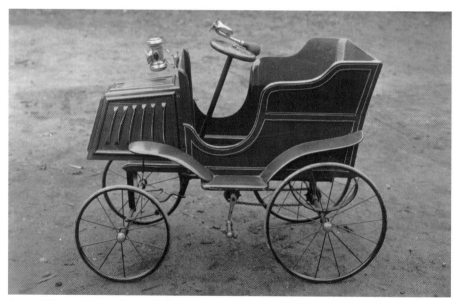

Any child would have been thrilled to own this early pedal car, while today it would be a collector's item. Built at Burton by Orton and Spooner, it was almost certainly converted from a stationary vehicle made for a fairground ride.

The First World War

The extensive Dixie sidings were normally used for sorting and marshalling wagons for the beer trade. General freight can still be seen, with reminders of some of the old railway companies, but shell cases have replaced barrels in this 1917 view.

Units of the Army Service Corps, concerned with supplies and transport, were quickly mobilized when war broke out. Burton, with its extensive railway facilities and many brewery premises available for storage and billeting, was a natural centre for ASC activity. The Corps became the RASC in 1918.

Many Burtonians joined local volunteer companies of the 6th Battalion, North Staffordshire Regiment and attended pre-war camps. 'You will recognise your big son filling his mattress' is the message sent to his mother by Sgt S.A. Elks.

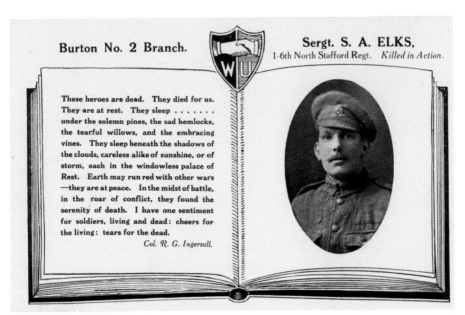

Burton No. 2 Branch.

Sergt. S. A. ELKS,
1-6th North Stafford Regt. *Killed in Action.*

These heroes are dead. They died for us. They are at rest. They sleep . . . . under the solemn pines, the sad hemlocks, the tearful willows, and the embracing vines. They sleep beneath the shadows of the clouds, careless alike of sunshine, or of storm, each in the windowless palace of Rest. Earth may run red with other wars —they are at peace. In the midst of battle, in the roar of conflict, they found the serenity of death. I have one sentiment for soldiers, living and dead: cheers for the living: tears for the dead.

Col. R. G. Ingersoll.

Sadly, the photo above was to be joined by another. The Workers' Union issued memorial cards of members who died fighting, one of whom was Sgt Elks.

Burton-on-Trent and District Prisoners of War Fund.

Mrs. LILY THOMAS,

Founder and Hon. Secretary of the Fund,

Who from February, 1915, to June, 1918, sent **16,120** Parcels to Burton Prisoners of War at a cost of **£7,000.**

Mrs Lily Thomas's wartime achievement on behalf of prisoners of war speaks for itself. She organized a vast amount of voluntary effort. From 1916 to 1918 she operated her parcels depot from a shop still standing in Main Street, Stapenhill, facing St Peter's Bridge. Mrs Thomas has modestly recorded the endeavours of herself and her helpers in a book entitled *Memories Grave and Gay.*

Lily Thomas with some returned Burton POWs who benefited from her efforts. She arranged dispatch of food and tobacco in over 5,000 parcels sent independently, and then 16,120 under the Red Cross scheme. R.H. Burt, postmaster, arranged for collections by handcart from her depot.

It is 31 October 1914 and war-time charities are already in action: Burton Girls' High School is performing in aid of the Belgian Relief Fund. Burton was a reception centre for Belgian refugees, some two hundred remaining throughout the war.

As more men joined the armed forces, women took over their jobs. Here they are handling a physically demanding task as ale loaders. The photograph is believed to be of Allsopp's brewery.

Perhaps less strenuous, this was still a new departure for women. Employees of Allsopp's paint shop pose in 1917 for a souvenir group photograph.

Photograph of an INCENDIARY BOMB found in Staffordshire after the Air Raid, January 31st, 1916.

These cards were sold after the 1916 Zeppelin raid showing the type of incendiary device dropped over the town. No town name appeared because of war-time censorship.

The amount realized from the Sale of these Cards to be given to the Fund in aid of the sufferers.

Territorial units were quickly in action and many Burtonians in this group became war casualties. This was C Squadron of the Staffordshire (Queen's Own Royal Regiment) Yeomanry under their commander, Major H.A. Clowes. Over 1,300 Burton men had died by 1918.

Burton Town Hall was commandeered as a Red Cross hospital. Miss Mary Thompson, Commandant, was awarded the OBE in 1918 and is the centre figure in this group of volunteers.

A Hospital fête held in July 1916 in the grounds of Burton Abbey. The photograph is inscribed on the back by R. Burns of the Royal Irish Fusiliers, who was a patient at the Red Cross hospital and is on the extreme right.

Stretcher bearers and wagons of the 6th Battalion, North Staffs crossing Trent Bridge on an exercise.

King Edward Place, 1919, when a tank inscribed 'Burtonia' was presented to the town. It was positioned at the town end of the Trent Bridge.

Peace Celebrations in *Burton-on-Trent.*

THE COMMITTEE on behalf of the Mayor, Corporation and Burgesses of the County Borough of Burton-on-Trent hopes to have the pleasure of seeing

Cpl. F. Archer,

at Lunch in the National Machine Gun Factory, Branstone Road, on Saturday, July 19th, 1919, at one o'clock, the date fixed for the Official Celebrations

of Peace.

On behalf of the Committee,

GEORGE HILL (Mayor) Chairman,

S. H. EVERSHED, Hon. Treasurer,

ARTHUR FOX, Hon. Secretary,

Corporal Archer's invitation to the Peace Celebrations, Saturday 19 July 1919. The National Machine Gun Factory was established at Branston in 1915 with American machinery, but the war ended before manufacturing commenced. In 1921 Crosse and Blackwell began production of Branston Pickle here, moving out later to be replaced by an artificial silk company. Before the Second World War the site became the Branston Ordnance Depot.

The Peace Celebration: the scene at Branston factory as ex-servicemen assemble for lunch. This was in two sittings after they had marched behind bands from the Grange Field. The day continued with a gala on the Ox-Hay ending with fireworks.

After the Armistice a temporary memorial was erected in the market-place for 11 November ceremonies. Burton's permanent war memorial was designed by H.C. Fehr and unveiled on 2 August 1922 by the Earl of Dartmouth.

MAY MORNING,
1916.

KEEP UP THE OLD CUSTOM.

Let your Comrades at the Front, who are so bravely fighting for King and Country, hear that those at home

Remembered them at this Service.

PREACHER:

The Rev. Canon Willink
(RECTOR OF BIRMINGHAM).

BE UP IN TIME!
Service 5 a.m.

This is the last time I shall appear at Holy Trinity Church as Vicar of the Parish. For 13 years I have tried to do my best for the Working Men and the Town of Burton. May God richly bless you all and give you peace.

H. TRAVIS BOULTBEE,

Vicar.

GOD SAVE THE KING.

[OVER.

The back of a photograph of the vicar of Holy Trinity church, 1916, announcing the unique 5 a.m. May Day morning service for brewery workers, which they could attend before going on shift. They had always attended in good numbers, receiving a buttonhole of spring flowers.

SECTION SEVEN

Around the Villages

The popular Bell Inn, Anslow, *c.* 1903. It was supplied by Evershed's brewery, which amalgamated with Marston and Thompson in 1905.

A Simnett reproduction from Sir Oswald Mosley's *History of Tutbury* (1832). The castle and Norman priory church are among East Staffordshire's greatest treasures. Tutbury developed around its castle – an iron-age hill fort, strengthened in Anglo-Saxon times and then turned into a Norman motte-and-bailey fortress. *Domesday Book* says, 'In the Borough around the castle are forty-two men who live only by their trading.' This is an unusual Domesday entry and it would be fascinating to know exactly how these men were occupied.

Glass cutting had begun in Tutbury by the early nineteenth century. Part of the works seen here stands on foundations of the cottage where Ann Moore lived. Her claim to have survived for six years without food attracted wide attention before her exposure as a fraud in 1813. This glass works is now Tutbury Crystal Glass Ltd, so both here and at Georgian Crystal (Tutbury) Ltd visitors can still see skilled local craftsmen at work. Tutbury post office still remains on the right-hand corner.

Branston village, 1904. A farm cart is passing the Smith's Arms on what was to become the A38 trunk road. Now the bypass has left Main Street as a cul-de-sac, with a rebuilt Blacksmith's Arms and new shops and houses replacing the old cottages seen here.

Playtime at Branston school, *c.* 1904. The teachers (from left) are thought to be Miss Phipps, Miss Roberts, Miss Siddals and one unknown, with the head teacher, James Hollyhead, in the shadows by the gate. A new school has replaced this building.

Wayside, a distinctive group of twenty-six houses, was built for employees when Crosse and Blackwell were at Branston factory in the 1920s. They remain, but the rural appearance of Burton Road is no more.

Children of Tatenhill enjoy the lucky dip at the chapel garden party sale on 19 July 1910 at the home of J.J. Newbold. This delightful period scene portrays the 'Sunday best' fashion of the day.

Sir Oswald Mosley, 4th Baronet (1848–1915) was both a public benefactor and prominent in local affairs. His residence, Rolleston Hall, was almost entirely demolished in 1926 when his son inherited the title. It was the 6th Baronet, his grandson of the same name, who became a political figure in the 1930s.

Sir Oswald made Rolleston Hall grounds available for organized outings, and this photograph suggests parental pride, as the children have been sent immaculately dressed, even with hats, for their school treat, around 1907.

Rolleston, c. 1904. Overlooking the brook are the village smithy of Henry Topley and the post and telegraph office, postmaster Arthur Williams. Letters were received at 6.50 a.m. and 3.20 p.m., and dispatched at 9.10 a.m. and 7.20 p.m. On Sundays letters could be posted at Rolleston station up to 7.20 p.m.

Tutbury was once a centre for wool stapling, then for silk. Later this cotton mill was built (in 1781) but the business moved to Rocester in 1888. Staton & Co. of Burton made it their plaster mill which served the gypsum industry until 1968. The site was then cleared and is now a picnic area.

With no traffic about you could swing your cart across the road for a good photograph. Oswald Parrick took over the grocery business of Henry Swinnerton, High Street, Tutbury, early in the century.

F.W. Scarratt, a Derby photographer, has captured the interest of local children to add to the charm of this Edwardian view of the Green, Barton-under-Needwood.

In May 1912 the Staffordshire Yeomanry held their fifteen-day annual training at Barton-under-Needwood, camping on Holt's field. Crowds watched contingents arriving (C Squadron marching from Burton), and activities were reported daily in the press. Here, one of the units has a break for refreshments.

Part of Rangemore Hall, Lord Burton's residence, seen beyond the cedar tree that King Edward VII planted during his house party visit in February 1902.

Greenhouse and garden staff at Rangemore Hall, *c.* 1906. Originally Sir Joseph Paxton of Chatsworth and Crystal Palace fame had landscaped the gardens and planned the conservatories and greenhouses, which in Lord Burton's time were noted for their many exotic fruits and flowers.

The King was again at Rangemore for a shoot on 20 November 1907. Seated on his pony in the centre he faces the camera. Fellow guests and beaters stand at a respectful distance. The generous supply of guns claimed 1,700 pheasants.

The Lord Burton memorial window in Rangemore church. Rangemore was a Victorian estate village with church, club, school and cottages all built by the Bass family.

Byrkley Lodge was the home of Hamar Bass, Lord Burton's brother. His son W.A.H. Bass inherited in 1898 and after Boer War service married Lady Noreen, a daughter of the Earl of Huntingdon, in 1903. The photograph records them and their handsome residence, which was demolished in 1953.

Local farmer Mr J.W. White gave Stretton the distinction of producing massive mangolds – aided by Hadfield's manure.

The second annual garden party of St Mary's church, Stretton, was held in the vicarage grounds on 6 July 1910, the Revd J. Edwards introducing Miss Gretton to open the event. Mr F. Attenborough, choirmaster and Burton music teacher, conducted the string orchestra. Winshill can just be discerned in the background.

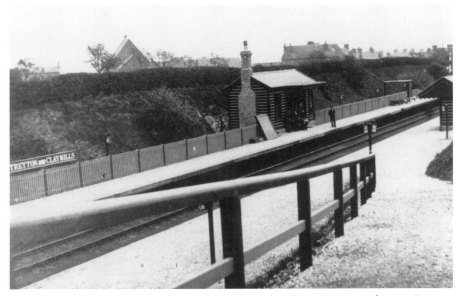

All three stations on the Burton to Tutbury line closed to passengers from 1 January 1949: Rolleston-on-Dove, Stretton and Clay Mills, and Horninglow. One mile apart, they had opened in 1894, 1901 and 1883 respectively. This is an early view of Stretton before the platforms were shortened, c. 1910.

A popular Edwardian comic postcard of the Tutbury Jenny, drawn and published by Cynicus, pseudonym of a Scottish artist, Martin Anderson. This design was widely adapted for local use.

Pleasure craft keep Barton lock busy today, but around 1902 the large building (now residential) was the Three Crowns Inn. The canal warehouse behind, where the landlord also handled coal and bricks, has also been tastefully converted for residential use, as Wharf Houses. The nearby Vine Inn has become the Barton Turns, but this once busy crossroads is now isolated from the main A38 trunk road.

SECTION EIGHT

Across the Trent

The Trent frozen, February 1929. Skating was possible over long stretches of the river. Removal of weirs to increase flow and the addition of heated water from power stations make a repetition unlikely, unless closure of power stations and promised colder winters again allow the skates to be brought out!

Stapenhill was still very much a country village when this ox-roast took place, at Mr Robinson's farm (now built over) in Woods Lane, to celebrate Queen Victoria's Diamond Jubilee in 1897. The occasion was a great success and 'the men were regaled right royally on Burton beer'. W. Grimsley immortalized it for us in 'A Poem For Stapenhill':

> John Wilkinson was Chairman, Fred Simnett was the Scribe;
> Will Inchbole was Committee man, who kept the lot alive;
> There were our village butchers and our village bakers too,
> And John, the village blacksmith, he joined the happy crew.

At the Stapenhill end of Ferry Bridge, through the still surviving arch inscribed Hill & Son's Ales, one entered the gardens of the original Punch Bowl Inn. Here you could enjoy strawberry teas, dancing, a small zoo – and concert parties like the Burton Pierrots, here using an outdoor stage at the rear of the butcher's shop of P.G. Ball.

Today's wide sweep out of Hill Street at Stapenhill makes it difficult to picture a fine tree on a bank high above Main Street. Local residents lined up for the camera to record it before removal around 1900.

The orchestra formed at St Peter's, Stapenhill in around 1910 by Captain Bonney of the Church Army. Back row, left to right: F. Wilson, Mrs Campion, Captain Bonney, Emmie Eyley, W. Brightman, Emmie Hood, H. Wilson, A. Bates. Front row: -?-, -?-, -?-, Miss Smith, Miss Smith, Miss Wilson.

The Revd Edwin Millard, curate at St Peter's, founded the League of Mercy for the protection of birds and animals. He organized lectures, lantern shows, a halfpenny magazine, and took members on outings to Dovedale.

Stapenhill Ladies Hockey Team in the mid-1920s was organized by Miss Meynell, the vicar's daughter, and they played on Vicarage Fields, now built over. Back row, left to right: May Barnett, Kathleen Sanders, Molly Sanders, Evelyn Burns. Second row: Winifred Bennett, Miss Meynell, Edna Lewis. Front row: Mollie Whitney, Maud Baldock, Sybil Hurley.

Stapenhill House was demolished in 1933 when the Pleasure Gardens were laid out, its former position marked by the sundial. This is the river frontage, only the steps remaining today.

Spring water was still used into the present century in Winshill, where even after piped water was introduced there were problems with pressure. Waterloo Clump water tower was built in 1904 to deal with this. The spring water here collects in an old cask to be used by cottagers of Brough Road, Hollow Lane and Berry Hedge Lane.

The rustic nature of pre-First World War Winshill village is well illustrated in this view at the corner of Berry Hedge Lane. The house on the left was formerly the thatched Old Gate Inn, with additional attractions in the adjoining Pleasure Grounds.

Greensmith's Mill, Newton Road, was a pre-Conquest site and a mill of Burton Abbey stood here. It has now ceased production but was noted for fine quality flour, and still utilized water power. This interior scene captured its old-time atmosphere.

Old Winshill families are recalled in this group of officials and judges at Winshill Flower Show on Lownd's field off Bearwood Hill Road, August 1912. Back row, left to right: -?-, G. Gibbs, F. Bradbury (both from Johnson's nurseries), W. Seaman (a wood carver at Spooner's), G. Bloor, A. Hood, a show judge from Rangemore Hall gardens, W. Morley, W. Holden, G. Mear. Second row: C. Howell, -?-, -?-, Francis Thompson (a Marston's director), J. Jakeman, W. Howse (both gardeners), F.G. Caulton (secretary and builder, nursing his son, Harold, who was very scared of photographer Simnett under his black cloth), W. Gibson (gardener), -?-. Front row: -?-, Gilbert Thompson (son of Francis Thompson, who became a director of Marston's and a Burton alderman), -?-. Young Harold was to become a Councillor and Mayor of Burton.

After Victorian development at the top of Mill Hill Lane, Winshill, there was very little additional building until the 1930s when renumbering on alternate sides also took place.

Until St Peter's Bridge opened in 1985 there was no road over the river between Trent Bridge and this one at Walton, built in the 1830s (a toll-bridge until 1901) to replace a ferry crossing. In turn it was replaced by the 'temporary' Bailey bridge (still in use), following flood damage shortly after the Second World War.

Three interesting Burton relics survive as ornamental features in the fernery at Newton Park. Here is an arch from the medieval Burton bridge and a pinnacle from the first Trinity church (1824–80). There is also a rebuilt portion of Burton Abbey gateway. There is no public access to these features.

Bladon Castle looks quite medieval with horses and carriage in the courtyard. Abraham Hoskins, a Burton solicitor, actually built it in the eighteenth century but in 1910 it was the residence of the Holbrooke family.

Hartshorne no longer has its mill (or furnace) pond to recall past industries. On the left there is now a restaurant in a renovated building, originally a corn mill and, from around 1800, a screw mill. The pool provided power for the water wheel but production ended in the mid-nineteenth century. The cottages were built for workers, but while those to the right have gone the Marston's inscription can still just be discerned.

An Edwardian multi-view of Bretby when the hall (a hospital from 1926) was a home of the Earl of Carnarvon (of Tutankhamun fame). Scenes include lodges, head-keeper's house and the church of 1878 which replaced an ancient building of around 1220.

Although certainly carefully posed, the scene above captures the popular conception of an old traditional farmyard in the days before barns, cowsheds and stables are converted into desirable residences. This is Dunnsmoor Farm, Hartshorne. Below, haymakers ride in J. Holmes's wagon, which has an extension frame for carrying high loads. Both scenes are within a mile or two of the coal and clay pits of the Swadlincote area.

Even in the middle of industrial spread the livestock market, seen here in around 1910, attracted considerable attention. In the background the bridge carries trams over the railway running into Swadlincote station. The post office now stands on this site in the centre of the town.

The edge of Swadlincote station platform is centre left. Kilns for the earthenware of Wragg's and Woodward's works can be seen beyond. The flat field, centre, was the 'Engine' ground for the town's cricket and football teams. On the right are the bottle kilns of Sharp's pottery.

Swadlincote Salvation Army Band at the Citadel, Wilmot Road, *c.* 1912. The standard bearer is Mr Jones. His son, Stanley, later had a record shop and his nephew played the organ on the QE2.

For many people Swadlincote meant Salt Bros, the popular stores that at different times occupied various premises in the High Street and were sadly missed when they closed. This 1920s view also shows another old established shop, H. Dinnis (left), jeweller and clockmaker, with Salt's clothing department adjoining.

A First World War photograph, probably taken at Newhall, in the style of a football team showing their trophies. These are employees of Warren, Stacey & Company, engineers and boiler-makers, one of whose war-time contracts was to cast trench howitzer shell cases.

During the 1912 pit strike many miners' families on 10s a week strike pay were in distress. This is inside Swadlincote Town Hall where a Relief Committee provided pea soup and currant pudding for miners' children.

'The light put to the bonfire by our dear sister Annie (Mrs John Perks) on Coronation Day of King George V and Queen Mary, Thursday June 22nd 1911. Photo taken by our nephew, Joseph Perks.' Perks was one of the district's best-known photographers, and this bonfire at Swadlincote was one of a string lit countrywide after a day of celebrations.

Dicken's Grocery, 53 High Street, Newhall, *c.* 1920. The shop was later owned by George Astle. Well-known brand names are on show but obviously there is a big drive on tinned tomatoes.

Linton Road at Castle Gresley with local children attracted by the photographer. Albert Eley, the grocer, is recommending Rowntree's cocoa, Symington's soups and Stephenson's furniture cream.

Just in view on the left is the last old cottage to survive in Swadlincote High Street. It was the original Bull's Head, the next building later becoming the inn. The cottage was demolished in 1935, Wroughton's shop replacing it. This scene was photographed in the early 1930s.

Woodville High Street, with tram No. 11 en route from Ashby to Burton, *c.* 1908. Looking up the hill from Belvedere Road corner, the Reliant Pottery chimney and Wesleyan church spire can be seen.

The Howard family of Bernard Street, Woodville, celebrate a double wedding at Granville Methodist church on 19 September 1918. Miss Winifred Howard was married to the Revd Thomas Sowerby (once serving at Gresley), who then officiated when Miss Victoria Howard married Sgt Leonard Hollingworth. Back row, left to right: -?-, Miss Hollingworth, Sgt Hollingworth, Revd T. Sowerby, Miss Sowerby, Mr Hollingworth, Mr H.M. Howard. Front row: Mrs Hollingworth, Constance Howard (later a local headmistress), Victoria, Howard Tooth, Winifred, Miss Howard (Beatie), Mrs Howard.

Castle Gresley brewery became Beard Bros and then Beard, Hill & Co. Ltd before being acquired by Marston's. The building then passed to Sustene Ltd, cattle food manufacturers, but in September 1914 an explosion and fire destroyed the works.

Popularly known as the Leicester Line Bridge (built by the Midland Railway and completed in 1849), many people felt that this should have been the location for Burton's second river crossing. In Edwardian times sailing was a favourite pastime 'above the weir' at Drakelow.

'Gresley Common before it became our park' is written on this photograph. From being an enclosed grass area for grazing the common had become a wilderness, partly the result of 'fedding' – extracting coal from shallow pits by a small 'federation' of miners. It was restored by Mr Herbert Lea as the Maurice Lea Memorial Park, and opened in 1929.

Union Road/Midland Road junction, looking towards Newhall, showing a Swadlincote Hospital gala procession of 1912 and a fairground. The colour light system (right) indicated occupancy of a single line section of the Ashby tramway.

The road from Woodville (called Wooden Box until 1847) down to Swadlincote showing Woodward's pipe works. Tubs to and from the huge open clay pit (left) used the incline to cross Coppice Side. This view is from around 1912, and demolition, reclamation and landscaping beginning in the 1960s have transformed this whole area, which now includes a ski centre.

A splendid period photograph recording Newhall residents at the corner of Sunnyside and Wood Lane around the turn of the century. While decorations suggest a celebration there is nothing to indicate a royal occasion. The small pennant (right) is inscribed 'Buller' so this may well be a Boer War triumph. After a period of humiliation for Britain, General Buller won acclaim with the Relief of Ladysmith in 1900. The shop window offers a good supply of celebratory liquid!

Cadley Colliery, Stanton, *c*. 1879. From left to right can be seen the shafts for Nos 3, 2 and 1 pits. The surface pony carried supplies to be sent underground. Seventh from left in the round cap is Alfred Thomas Clamp as a young man.

Over forty years later Mr Clamp, the engine-wright, appears on the extreme left of this Cadley scene taken during the 1921 or 1926 pit strike. His son, Alfred Lawrence, is on the right; the pit manager is in the centre. The police officers were drafted in for security purposes.

Incongruously prominent in the background is a fascinating weathervane of a man with gun and dog, but this fine scene represents an epitaph for a lost industry. The once thriving collieries of South Derbyshire and North Leicestershire are now all closed with, often, few traces left of the sites or only the temporary scars of open cast mining

remaining. This Richard Keene photograph, full of fascinating detail, is typical of what was once an everyday scene at Stanton, Bretby, Newhall, Swadlincote, Gresley, Linton, Donisthorpe, Moira, Netherseal, Measham . . .

Acknowledgements

This book is almost completely compiled from the authors' own collections. We are, however, indebted to those people who, over many years, have given or allowed us to copy local scenes now included here. For loan of pictures, help in identification or for providing invaluable information and source material we particularly wish to thank the following:

Bass Museum • Charles Boyce • Tony Brenan • *Burton Daily Mail*
Burton Public Library • S.G. Clamp • Charles Holden • Philip Kenny
Alf Moss • Denis Stuart • Mrs Gladys Thompson • Ben Ward • Peter White.